W9-CBP-844

Baptist Beliefs

By E. Y. MULLINS, D.D., LL.D.

VALLEY FORGE
JUDSON PRESS®

CONTENTS.

BAPTIST BELIEFS.

A creed is like a crystal with many angles and facets. As the crystal is formed in obedience to natural law, so a creed is formed in obedience to a spiritual law. Michael Angelo chiseled the marble into the heroic figure of Moses as the expression of his artistic vision. The great creeds are the chiseled results of spiritual vision. What men see and feel they must express. Doctrinal statements are given exact form for the same reason an Indian makes his arrow straight and sharp. Both are designed as weapons, or implements to achieve results.

This is not written as a formal creed. If so it would be much more condensed. A very few sentences at most would be sufficient for each article. But there are a number of excellent Baptist creeds in existence already, and what is proposed here is not the setting up

of another, but rather a restatement and interpretation for the general reader of those now
in existence and in common use among us.
An effort is made to avoid technical theological
terms as far as possible to provide the simplest
and clearest statement. There are, of course,
many topics touched upon in the pages which
follow where the paths of discussion lead in
various directions. We are required by the
limited scope of our undertaking, however, to
abstain from too elaborate treatment of any
subject. A general survey of the beliefs com-
monly held by Baptists with the necessary
cross lines to mark off the sub-divisions of
teaching clearly and distinctly is all we can
hope to accomplish within our prescribed limits.

One caution is needed at the outset. Creeds
are very valuable when used properly, but,
like all other good things, dangerous when
used otherwise. Creeds are the natural and
normal expression of the religious life. The
right to make them is nothing more nor less
than the divinely given right to think. He
who would forbid men to make creeds expressive of their own religious life in the light of
Bible teaching, would therein forbid the free
exercise of human freedom to think. But observe this point: creeds are the expression of
religious life, of vital or living experience.
The great creeds which have powerfully in-
fluenced the life of mankind have all arisen

in periods of great religious energy and deep
religious experience. They are like lava
which comes hot from the volcano. An inner
power expels them. The lava cools afterward.
The creed tends to become stereotyped and
formal.

There is another truth which must always
be kept in mind. The right to make creeds
is simply another way of saying that we have
no right to enforce them upon men against
their wills. The voluntary principle is at the
heart of Christianity. The right of private
judgment in religion is a right which lies at
the core of Christian truth. The right of A
to make a creed expressive of his own religious
life implies the right of B to make his own
creed as well. It would be tyranny to
forbid A to make his creed, and it would
be equal tyranny to compel or attempt
to compel B to accept the creed of A. If A
and B should by voluntary co-operation come
to see alike and thus adopt the same creed
there would be no tyranny. And if A and B
and any number of others should thus set forth
their beliefs for all the world to understand,
this would be simply the exercise of their freedom in Christ. And this is precisely the way
Baptist creeds and confessions of faith have
arisen. No Baptist creed can be set up as final
and authoritative apart from the Scriptures.
They are all subject to revision when-
ever and wherever other Baptists see fit to

make a fresh statement of their doctrinal beliefs. Of course, Baptists have a right to the peaceful exercise of their freedom in holding and maintaining their own views as to Christian truth. In this the group or denomination corresponds to the individual in the matter of freedom. Consequently they themselves must judge when an individual or group within the larger body has departed from the common view sufficiently to warrant separation. The enforced continuance of an individual with the larger group after radical and hopeless divergence of belief has arisen is a tyranny equal with the enforcement of the beliefs of the group upon the individual. Religious freedom, in other words, is a right of the group as well as of the individual. The voluntary principle applies equally and alike to both. It is on this principle indeed that most of the denominations since the Reformation have come into existence. Denominationalism is the result of the right of private judgment in religion. A Baptist should be the last man in the world to question the right of a Presbyterian, Methodist or any other, to the full and free exercise of his right of private judgment in religion. If denominationalism ever ceases to exist and all Christians become one it will be not by means of artificial schemes of union, but through the gradual growth of unity of view, that is, through the operation of the voluntary principle.

Another peril of creeds is that we shall mistake the shell for the kernel, the form for the life. Creeds that are forged when religious life is at white heat may remain after the fire has gone out. The creed without the life then becomes a chain to bind, not wings on which the soul may fly. The one and only remedy, then, is to return to Christ and kindle the flame of religion once more. Creeds are useful only so long as they are the normal expression of life and are used as a means of propagating life. To hold a creed as intellectually true merely, without the inner life and power, is not a religious act at all. The New Testament knows nothing whatever of any such holding of creeds and we would do well to reject all creeds and go straight to the New Testament rather than lapse into a barren intellectualism through a dead creed. The danger is so great that this barren intellectualism will arise, or that creeds will be employed as whips to coerce men into uniformity of belief by carnally-minded champions of the faith, that many Baptists exercise their freedom by having nothing to do with creeds, or rather by repudiating all of them, and looking to the Scriptures alone for their doctrinal beliefs. Here, again, they are strictly within their rights as freemen in Christ. Nevertheless, I think creeds perform a useful function in educating us to unity of faith and practice, so long as they are not worn as death masks for

defunct religion, or employed as lashes to
chastise others; so long as they do not arrest
life and growth—in short, creeds help rather
than hinder. A creed is like a ladder. On it
you may climb up to a lofty outlook, a purer
spiritual atmosphere, or you may climb down
to the low platform of a barren orthodoxy.

In this spirit the following pages are written. The author has no sort of thought that
his statement is the best that can be made, or
in any sense final. Others will improve on
these statements and we shall come more and
more to a clear understanding of the meaning
of the Bible and of the religion of Christ.

THE SCRIPTURES.

There are three marks which in a general
way may be said to sum up the position of the
Scriptures in the belief of Baptists. The first
is sufficiency. The Scriptures give us enough
truth for all religious purposes. Nature re-
flects the divine attributes to a certain extent
and, according to Paul, if men should actually
live up to the light of nature within, in conscience, and without, in the universe, they
might arrive at a knowledge of God, so that
they are without excuse. For, owing to their
naturally evil bent, men refuse to follow the
light of nature (Romans 1:19-21). Taking
men as they are, therefore, on account of sin,
the light of nature is insufficient. A revela-

tion of God to them and a coming of God into
their lives are the only means for their redemption. In the Scriptures we have all the
truth required for the religious life of men.

Another quality of the Scriptures which fits
them to serve as the source of light and truth
in religion is certainty. There are greater or
less degrees of certainty in science and philosophy. Yet scientific and philosophic theories
are always subject to revision. Science does
attain to permanent truth. But this truth of
science is not religious truth at all, save in the
general sense that all truth is of God. The
laws of nature, like the law of gravitation, or
the laws of motion, or the laws of chemical
affinity, for example, have no direct religious
value at all. None of them can save the soul.
Physical science, indeed, ends where religion
begins, viz., at the realm of spirit and of personal fellowship between God and man. Physical science cannot prove or disprove the soul's
immortality or the existence of God. Philosophy, in like manner, fails to prove, as religion
requires, the great truths of human life and
destiny. Philosophy gives us a set of rational
theories of the world, some of which include a
belief in God, and some of which do not. Each
theory or world view of philosophy selects
some one thing, matter, or motion, or mind, or
will, or personality, or something else, and de-
duces all the rest from that. But so long as
men are at liberty to select these various things

on which to build their philosophies there will be as many kinds of philosophy as there are preferences among men. No one philosopher can compel the others to select his own starting point, any more than one woman can require other women to agree with her taste as to the most beautiful shade of silk or shape of hat. Hence we repeat, philosophy does not yield certainty in religion. The Bible does. The Bible tells us how to find God and by following its directions we actually find him. God comes into our life and we know beyond a peradventure that the Bible speaks to us truly concerning God.

The third quality of the Scriptures is authoritativeness. The Scriptures speak with authority, as does no other literature in the world. This authoritative note which rings so clear in the Bible is not due to anything external to itself. No court made it authoritative by decree. No church council made it so by decision. No pope made it so by hurling anathemas at those who denied it. The early church councils in the second, third and fourth centuries did not make the Bible authoritative. They simply recognized the authority of the Book itself. The canon of Scripture under God took care of itself. It was inevitable that this dynamic and mighty literature would come together in a vital and organic unity since it was all created by one common life and power of God.

Behind this sufficiency and authoritativeness of the Scriptures of the Old and New Testaments is their inspiration. Holy men of God spoke as they were moved by the Holy Spirit. There are many ways of explaining the method of inspiration which men have adopted. We cannot here discuss them. The fact is the supreme thing. The Bible is God's message to man given to supply the needs of his religious life. When we find that message we have God's truth to us which is all we need for religious knowledge, faith and obedience.

The process of inspiration is necessarily more or less mysterious and obscure, since it is God's act through his Spirit stooping to the plane of the human intellect and experience and employing these as channels of truth to other men. Someone has compared this act of condescension on God's part to the slightly stooping statue of a beautiful woman found in a European art collection. By no process of measurements has it been possible to determine just how much below the height of the erect figure the stooping statue measures. In like manner we are without any power to determine precisely how God adapts himself to human capacity in the process of inspiration. The result, however, we possess in the oracles of the Scriptures, and these serve all our practical religious needs and ends.

The Bible is the book of religion. Let us keep this in mind. It is a mistake to think

of it as a text-book on science or any other
subject except religion. In conveying religious
truth the writers of the Bible could only gain
a hearing for their inspired religious message
by employing the means of conveying ideas in
common use. It is astonishing, indeed, how
the Bible statements conform broadly and generally to the teachings of science. But the
biblical writers had to use the language of ap-
pearances, of things as they looked to the ordinary eye, not the language of exact science.
Suppose Job, for example, had been inspired
to use the Newtonian law of gravitation in his
debate with his friends, would it have helped
out the argument? Would it not rather have
discredited him more than ever?

The law of gravitation as stated by exact
science is that bodies attract each other directly as the mass and inversely as the square
of the distance. Now we can imagine the
Spirit of God revealing this to Job. But it
implies the whole of modern astronomy with
its Copernican view of the universe. It came
as the result of careful and painstaking ex-
periment and calculation. His friends would
have been unconvinced by it had Job employed
it. It would have been to them an unknown
tongue, save as the result of a miracle of revelation to them also, enabling them to antici-
pate the researches of science thousands of
years. And this indicates clearly how God re-
fuses to rob man of his own proper task of re-

search and discovery by miracles of revelation concerning physical matters. The Bible was not meant to teach us "how the heavens go, but how to go to Heaven". Job would therefore probably have discredited his own message had he sought to become a channel for the communication of a knowledge of the laws of astronomy in the scientific sense.

The man of today makes a similar mistake when he stakes the integrity and authoritativeness of the Bible on its exact agreement with the Newtonian law of gravitation or the Copernican astronomy. The Bible is not a book of science. It is a book of religion.

The Bible must be interpreted. But we have for our illumination in interpreting the same Spirit who inspired it. Everything in the Bible is not equally binding on us, because wicked men speak, Pharaoh, Judas, the devil. We must get God's message by interpreting under the Spirit's guidance. There are parables and allegories and symbols; literal and highly picturesque statements; and there are writers with varied individualities and points of view. There is progress from less to more of truth. God gave the truth gradually. In all these ways the necessity for interpretation is upon us. It is a great and high responsibility, but we cannot evade it, and we cannot know what God's message to us is until we have interpreted it and made due allowance for all the facts which have been named. But when we have found out what the Bible means to say to us we have the truth.

We may sum up all by saying the Bible culminates in Christ. He is the crown of the whole. All doctrine before and after Christ must be seen in the light which shines from him if we are to understand it. Christ, then, is God's message to us and we are to understand the whole Bible simply and solely in its relations to Jesus Christ, the Son of God and Savior of the world.

2 Timothy 3:15-17; Luke 16:29-31; Ephesians 2:20; 2 Peter 1: 19-21; Romans 15:4; Hebrews 1:1, 2; Psalms 19:7, 8; Romans 1:19-21; 1 John 5:9; Romans 3:1,2; John 16:13; 15:26, 27; 14:25, 26; 1 Corinthians 2:4, 10, 11, 12, 13, 14, 15, 16; 1 John 2:20, 27; John 6:45; 1 Corinthians 14:26; 2 Peter 3:16; Psalm 119:130; Isaiah 8:20; Acts 15:15; John 5:39; 1 Corinthians 14:6, 9, 11, 12, 24, 28; Colossians 3:16; Matthew 22:29; Acts 28:23.

GOD.

It is impossible to define God, because he is more and greater than all definitions. This does not mean that we must remain ignorant of God's character. For we do possess most real knowledge of God through the revelation he has given us in grace and power in our hearts and lives. There are certain qualities or attributes which we ascribe to God in consequence of his revelations in nature and in experience and in Scripture. These must not be taken as if they were exhaustive statements of what God is either himself or in his manifestations. First, we say God is a spiritual being. Jesus said to the woman at the well, "God is spirit, and they that worship him must worship him in spirit and in truth." This is, we may say, the first truth in spiritual religion. God has not a visible outward form or figure. He is pure spirit.

It is curious how many people fail to grasp the idea of God's spirituality and cling to the pictures of him learned in the nursery. The writer has met several adults, among them students in theology, who had difficulty in overcoming the physical way of representing God. Some think of him as a very wise old man with gray hair and beard sitting above the world on a great throne, or else they cling to other more or less vague and misty pictures of God under various human forms. It is very necessary that we grasp the idea of God's spirituality and nearness, his omnipresence and power in our lives if we are to walk with him as we should.

Again God is one. There are not many gods, but only the one true God. The doctrine of many gods is polytheism and against it the prophets of the Old Testament poured out their inspired and burning eloquence. The Old Testament is the record of how God trained Israel to the thought of a pure monotheism, that is, to the belief in one holy and spiritual God. The unity of God is another of the first truths of religion.

God is personal. Some modern theories seek
to enforce the idea of an impersonal God, or,
in the current expression, an impersonal
"world-ground". This thought of an impersonal ground of the world grows out of the
thought of substance which science uses in its
dealings with nature. It is sought to reduce
all things to one physical principle in order
to explain scientifically everything that exists.
But the impersonal substance is not God. Religion teaches, and most of all Christianity
teaches, that God is above as well as in nature;
that nature and substance, while the expression of God's wisdom and power are not God
himself. Religion dies when God ceases to be
personal in the thoughts of men, because everything in religion requires a personal God. It
is not surprising, then, that when men forsake
the idea of a personal God they lapse into
polytheism and invent many gods, or else they
adopt the philosophy of pantheism instead of
religion, and remain content with that.

Again, God is holy. The moral law is
grounded in God. He is its author and is
himself clothed with all moral perfections.

God is infinite. This means that God is
free of all imperfections. Our minds cannot
grasp the infinite fully. The word is negative in the sense that it seeks to express the
thought that God has no limitations of any
kind. God, then, is infinite in all his at-

tributes—wisdom, holiness, love, power and all
others which may be named.

The Scriptures also reveal to us that God
manifests himself to men not only as one but
as triune. In the Old Testament God's Spirit
appears in many forms of activity, although
the Trinity does not appear in the Old Testament as a fully developed truth as in the New.
The New Testament clearly shows that there
are three forms of God's personal manifestation in the world, called Father, Son and Holy
Spirit. This does not mean that God shows
himself as first one, then another of these. They
are distinct in their personal activities. Of
course, when we call them persons we
do not use the word in its ordinary
sense. A human person is a separate and distinct individual and if we use the word in
this meaning referring to the Trinity we would
imply three gods, which would be polytheism.
Yet personality is the most fitting word we
can find to express the truth as to the Trinity.

The Bible does not explain the Trinity. It
simply gives us the facts. Theologians and
philosophers have tried hard to give an intellectual expression to the doctrine of the Trinity. None of them have succeeded fully. Some
of them have been very elaborate and have
attempted entirely too much perhaps. Nevertheless we must accord them the right to make
these attempts. It will probably be found in
the end, however, that the briefer the defini-

tion of the Trinity the better for practical purposes. God is revealed to us as Father, Son and Holy Spirit. These have personal qualities. Yet God is one. This is the New Testament teaching. Beyond this we tend toward speculation.

Exodus 15:11; Psalm 147:5; Psalm 83:18; Isaiah 6:3; 1 Peter 1:15, 16; Mark 12:30; Matthew 10:37; Matthew 28: 19; 1 Corinthians 12:4-6; 1 John 5:7; John 10:30; John 5:17; John 4:24; Ephesians 2:18; 2 Corinthians 13:14.

PROVIDENCE.

God who created the world upholds it. In the ongoing of the world there are no surprises to God. He foresees and foreknows all things whatsoever which may or can or do take place. God is above the world but he is also in it. He does not hold himself aloof from his universe and watch its movements as if it were merely a machine. He is present in it everywhere at all times. He is in and through and above all things.

God's purpose includes all things which come to pass. Some things, however, God simply permits. God is not the author of sin. It entered the world not by his approval but only by his permission. Yet he overrules it. Somehow the possibility of sin was connected with the freedom of God's intelligent creatures. It is this freedom which lifts men above the brutes. Yet it was this same freedom which made possible a sinful choice. That sinful choice in like manner made possible a display of God's love and grace which could not have appeared in a non-sinning universe. This does not condone sin; it simply indicates how God transformed it into an occasion for boundless condescension and love.

Most of the difficulties about God's grace and human freedom are due to the prevalent way of thinking about grace and its action upon us. Grace comes from without, but it acts within us. It flows in as it were and works itself out through our minds, consciences and wills. It moves us freely. It inclines us to act voluntarily as God wills. It is not like a crowbar resting on a fulcrum by means of which a stone is moved. It is rather like water in a millrace filling the receptacles on the rim and turning the wheel. Our faculties are the receptacles on the wheel of our personality. Or again, grace is like the sap in a tree, and our conduct is like the fruit. The fruit is produced from within. Grace is not mechanical, but personal in its action. This distinction explains hardshellism. Preaching, persuasion, missions, evangelism, are all based on the principle that grace is not a mechanical but a personal force. If grace were a crowbar and men stones, hardshellism would be right. It is the crowbar conception of grace that destroys missions. Grace works with those means which influence the free choices of men, persuasion,

argument, appeal, warning, exhortation, etc.
The whole New Testament conception of
preaching grows out of the fact that grace is
a personal, not a mechanical, force. Ideas,
feelings, volitions in the preacher through
God's Spirit, awaken ideas, feelings, volitions
in the sinner. This is the method of grace.
A bulb may have sleeping in it the potentiali-
ties of a beautiful flower. Something from
without must enter it, however, before it can
ever become a flower, something it does not
possess, viz., the sunlight and its warmth.
Transferring the bulb from one basket to another would not bring out the flower. The
Spirit of God must enter and change the sinner's heart before the slumbering possibilities
can be brought forth. It is the unfolding of
his personality into moral and spiritual life
which is the aim of the Gospel. This can only
be accomplished as the living personality of
one man becomes in some way the medium
through which the truth and grace and power
of God enters the life of another. At least
this is God's ordinary method, whatever may
be true in exceptional cases like that of Saul
of Tarsus and others.

God made man free and leaves him free.
God never overrides the will of man. In his
action upon man's will he always respects that
will. "Irresistible grace" is a phrase we sometimes hear. But properly understood it never
means irresistible in the physical sense, as if

God dealt with us as a parent might with a
crying and disobedient and rebellious child in
lifting it bodily and carrying it where the
child refused to go. God will have us come
to him freely. Grace always persuades and
convinces and makes us willing to come, however mysterious and mighty it may be in its
action upon our hearts.

The crown of God's creation is man. All
the previous stages led up to this being who
was made in the image and likeness of God.
This is the chief interest of religion in the
wonder and mystery of creation. The question of how God created the world, or how
long it has been since the creation of man, are
questions which are not fully answered in the
Scriptures. Science is at work on them and
may or may not succeed in answering these
questions fully. The book of Genesis contains
light on some points, but not all. One thing
is clear, however, and that is that God made
man in his own image and that man sinned.
Another point is clear and that is that the
redemption of sinful man is the center of
God's providential care of the world. If we
would understand providence then we must
study what God has done to redeem the world.

Genesis, chapters 1 and 2; John 1:2,3; Romans 1:20;
Hebrews 1:2; Job 26:13; Colossians 1:16; Romans
2:14-16; Isaiah 46:10, 11; Psalm 135:6; Ephesians 1:11;
Acts 2:23, 24; Acts 7:1-60; Acts 14: 16-18; Acts 17:24-
28.

THE FALL OF MAN.

The meaning of the fall of man is that man sinned against God. Sin is not human infirmity merely, nor is it a mistake merely, nor is it ignorance merely. Sin, again, is not merely a step upward in man's evolution towards his highest development. The fall was a downward and not an upward movement of man. It involved guilt and transgression. It gave rise to the need of pardon, of grace and redemption. Man came under condemnation as the result of his fall. The fall, then, means that man was really man when he fell and not merely a creature who was on his way towards becoming man, a candidate, as it were, for manhood. Of course, we are not to suppose he possessed all that has come to man in man's struggle, nor all the experience or knowledge which history has brought. Man was not made omniscient, nor even learned in the modern sense. He was made free from sin and condemnation, and through the temptation of Satan he fell.

In consequence of the fall of man sin has become hereditary. No teaching of science is clearer today than the hereditary transmission of traits of character. The Old Testament gave religious recognition to the principle long before science discovered and demonstrated it. As a result of this sinful heredity of race, all men actually sin when they acquire capacity

6 2 3 8 1

for sinning. We believe that infants dying in infancy are saved not because they have no share in the operation of the hereditary tendency to sin, but because Christ atoned for all the race, and somehow children dying in infancy, before actual sin, share in the blessing of that atonement. The Scriptures really say little of the salvation of infants dying in infancy, but they say enough to warrant firm belief in that salvation. The grace of God deals with them in a special manner, no doubt, as we must hold if we believe in hereditary sin and at the same time in the salvation of infants dying in infancy.

No one is or can be saved without repentance and faith, who is capable of exercising repentance and faith. This is the clear teaching of the Scriptures. Hereditary and actual sin render men not only corrupt but also guilty and condemned until they are justified by faith in Jesus Christ.

All men are not equally sinful, of course, and no man is as bad as he can be. But all man's faculties and powers are affected by the operation of sin in his nature, and all are equally incapable of saving themselves. All are dependent alike upon God's grace for salvation.

Genesis 1:31; Genesis 2:16, 17; Genesis 3:12, 18; Genesis 3:6-24; Romans 3:23; Genesis 6:5; Titus 1:15; Romans 3:10-18; Romans 8:7; Romans 1:18-32; Romans 5:12-21; Galatians 5:16-21; Isaiah 53:6; Ephesians 2:1-3; Ezekiel 18:19,20.

ELECTION.

In consequence of their sinful nature and habitual choice of evil, men, if left to themselves, would inevitably refuse salvation. A Gospel, or good news of salvation, announced to a race of sinful men and left without the active energy of God's grace to make it effectual, would surely come to naught. There are two choices necessary in a man's salvation: God's choice of the man and man's choice of God. Apart from infants and others incapable of responding to the Gospel call, salvation never comes otherwise than through God's choice of man and man's choice of God. But God's choice of man is prior to man's choice of God, since God is infinite in wisdom and knowledge, and since he will not make the success of his Kingdom dependent on the contingent choices of men. God does not fling out the possibility of salvation among men, say, like a golden apple, and leave it for men to use or not use as they will. He keeps his own hands on the reins of his government. Yet in doing so he must needs observe his own law of freedom as written in man's moral constitution. This is the problem and task which calls for infinite wisdom, love and power: To save man and yet leave man free to choose salvation. Free-will in man is as fundamental a truth as any other in the Gospel and must never be canceled in our doctrinal statements. Man would not be man without it and God never robs us of our true moral manhood in saving us.

In dealing with a race of beings who, if left to themselves, would inevitably choose evil, and yet whose freedom must be respected, how else could God act in saving them than as he has acted, viz., in not only sending his Son as Mediator and Redeemer, but also in devising means and instrumentalities for persuading men to believe and accept the Gospel. If he should pick them up bodily, as it were, and force salvation upon them against their wills, he would do an immoral thing. Indeed, such a method is inconceivable with free beings. Yet if God holds aloof from men and merely awaits their choice of him, none would choose him. The Gospel, the Holy Spirit, the church, the preacher, the message or sermon, and all other means of persuading and inclining men to believe are, therefore, necessary in order that God may save, first, because he has chosen man, and second, through man's choice of God. The decree of salvation must be looked at as a whole to understand it. Some have looked at God's choice alone and ignored the means and the necessary choice on man's part. Others have ignored God's choice and have made all depend on the means and man's choice. But you cannot split up the decree of God into little bits and understand it by looking at the pieces. You must view it as a whole.

Election is sometimes said to indicate arbitrariness and partiality in God. But this is an error. God wills that all men should be saved and come to a knowledge of the truth (1 Timothy 2:4), as Paul assured us. Certainly Jesus died for the whole world (John 3:16). Election is not an arbitrary choice on God's part. Infinite love is behind his every act. He adopts the only method by which the salvation of any would be possible, and no doubt he yearns for and desires that as rapidly as possible all men should hear and know the truth and obey it. This is why he chooses men not merely to salvation but to service. Every saved man or woman or child is intended by God as a messenger and worker to make known his grace and power to others.

Election leaves no room for boasting or pride or sense of merit on our part, but it does, when truly understood, fill us with humility and a sense of the manifold wisdom of God in dealing with his free creatures. And it should inspire us with a holy sympathy with God in his effort to save men who are disobedient and rebellious and carnal in their choices. With God we may, then, patiently co-operate in persuading men to believe the Gospel, in the full assurance that God's grace will prove equal to the great task of leading even the rebellious to forsake their sins and freely choose him;

and that the energetic action of God's holy
will in a world held even in the grip of hereditary sin will be efficacious in redeeming men
and establishing among them his eternal Kingdom.   We should be hopeless in our labors if
the outcome of our efforts were contingent
upon the unaided response of sinful men.   All
uncertainty vanishes, however, in the full persuasion, warranted by the Scriptures that God
guides, controls and efficaciously wills the glorious outcome.

Acts 13:48; Exodus 33:18, 19; Matthew 20:15; Ephesians 1:3-14; 2 Timothy 1:8, 9; 1 Peter 1:1, 2; 2 Thessalonians 2: 13, 14; 1 Corinthians 4:7; 1 Corinthians
1:27; 1 Thessalonians 2:12, 13; 2 Timothy 2:10; John
6:37-40; 1 Thessalonians 1:4-10; 2 Peter 1:10, 11; Hebrews 6:11; Acts 4:27, 28; Numbers 23:19; 1 Timothy
5: 21; John 10:25-29; Romans 9:19-33.

THE MEDIATOR.

There is one Mediator between God and
man, Jesus Christ.   He was born of the Virgin
Mary through the power of the Holy Spirit.
He lived a sinless life; taught perfectly the
truth about God and human destiny; was himself the true manifestation of God in the flesh;
died on the cross and atoned for the sins of
men; was buried; rose again from the dead;
appeared to the disciples; ascended to the right
hand of the Father, and gave the Holy Spirit
to his people.   He now presides over the des-

tinies of his church and will come again at the time appointed by the Father to judge the world.

Two or three points call for special emphasis. Attempts are often made in our day to hold that Jesus was the first true revealer of God in conjunction with the other view that in no sense did he transcend the human. This is a favorite view with many who feel that science forbids them to accept the true divinity or deity of Jesus. They would make of him simply the greatest of the prophets or the greatest of the saints, but as such they think that he brings us the true knowledge of God. If men insist on applying the criterion of physical law to religion, however, they can never prove the existence of God even. For the laws of nature come to an end when we rise above nature into the realm of persons, and especially when we come to deal with the divine person. Science explains horizontally or on a level, we may say. The cause of every effect in physical nature lies behind the effect on the same level. The series of causes and effects in nature is like a row of bricks. Knock over the first brick in the row and in turn each of the others will be knocked over. Nothing is explained in nature save as we assign something we know to explain a new and unknown thing. The effect must be explained in terms of the cause. A brick must be explained by another brick. This is the meaning of the law of the transformation of energy or physical causation. If nature is a row of bricks, then we never find a God in nature, but only an endless row of bricks. This I say is the way science treats nature. Science, therefore, never can prove or disprove God's existence. It is difficult to see how men can accept the testimony of Jesus as to what God is unless they admit that he reveals God not merely from the human but also from the divine side. Jesus was not merely the "Prince of Saints", as Martineau has called him. He could not be a revealer of God in the full sense of the word unless he was more than the chief of saints. We would seem to be left with no sure knowledge of God, therefore, unless Jesus was more than a man. For science never demonstrates God, and the experience of even the greatest of saints would always be open to question when he attempted to convey to us a knowledge of the infinite God. As limited and human in mental capacity his experience might be perfectly genuine, but the rigidly scientific objector could always raise a question as to whether the explanation of the experience was the true and correct one. To himself the explanation might be perfectly satisfactory, but so long as the objector could question his capacity to grasp the infinite and convey an adequate revelation of God, his testimony would find limited acceptance. If Jesus, then,

was a genuine and final revelation of God to
men, he must have been more than a man
reaching up and seeking to find God. He
must also have been God coming down among
men and making himself known to them.
And this is precisely the testimony of the
Scriptures, so that in Jesus Christ we have the
true revelation of God to man.

Christ's atonement was necessary for the
pardon, justification and redemption of sinners.
There are many theories of the atonement,
too many for discussion here. They may easily be grouped into two classes: First, those
which make Christ's work on the cross terminate on men only; and, second, those which
make it terminate also on God. The latter
is the true view. God, indeed, was not induced
to love men by what Christ did. He loved
them beforehand, and Christ's work was the
expression and proof of his love. It was not
that God was an unwilling tyrant who had to
be bought over to man's side by the shedding
of Christ's blood. The atonement was God's
own arrangement and provision to meet an
infinite necessity of his holy and loving nature.
God set forth Christ to be the propitiation for
our sin in order that he might be both just
and the justifier of him who believeth in Jesus
Christ.

It is sometimes argued that this idea of an
objective or substitutionary atonement, something done by Christ, which is the ground

of the remission of sins, is not a part of the true Gospel of Christ, but was a bit of Judaism brought over into Christ's true Gospel by Paul, who was originally a Jew. This is a very inconsistent view of Paul. For it is very generally recognized that Paul was the one apostle who fully escaped the narrow trammels of Judaism and grasped fully the universalism of the Gospel. In particular it is Paul's doctrine of justification by faith which revolutionized Judaism, or rather overthrew it completely, and showed that the Gospel was as wide as the world in its meaning and intention. This, I say, is quite generally admitted. And yet there are those who allege that wrapped up with Paul's universal doctrine which killed Judaism, is an essential part of Judaism which would kill the Gospel, viz., his doctrine of an objective atonement. Paul certainly thought of his doctrine in the main as the direct antithesis and contradiction of Judaism. In part indeed it was the fulfillment of Judaism, but in that fulfillment Judaism was abolished. Paul's doctrine of atonement, then, is not an alien element in the Gospel. Jesus himself predicted that he would give his life a ransom for many (Matt. 20:28) and that he would shed his blood for the remission of sins (Matt. 26:28). The Scriptures indeed refrain from philosophizing about the atonement, but they set forth the truth in such terms that we cannot truly say that we are left entirely in the

3

dark as to how Christ's death saves us. The
holiness of God no less than his love required
the atoning work of Jesus. It is a false method
which separates one attribute of God, such as
his love, from other attributes, and asserts
that God acted in a part of his nature only in
his approach to men in the atoning work of
Jesus. God acted always as a unit, in his
entire nature, not in a fragment of it.

From the fact that other religions including
Judaism have in them the idea of sacrifice
and propitiation, it is concluded by some that
it must be a false idea. Fundamentally this
assumes that everything in the non-Christian
religions must be wholly false. Is it not far
more likely that a universal religious idea has
in it an element of truth than that its univer-
sality is a mark of its falsity? Christianity
purified and fufilled all religious ideas of men,
emptied them of their transient and superficial
meanings and revealed their true inward meaning. The atonement of Christ in a very special manner does this. In it God appears in
Christ, not as a distant, implacable and angry
being, requiring a satisfaction for sin which
man cannot supply. He himself, as holy and
loving and yearning to save men, provides the
satisfaction.

Christian experience through the ages has
given a hearty amen to the substitutionary
atonement of Christ. The sinner knows well that
it answers exactly his need so soon as he begins

to reflect upon and repent of his sins.   Dr.
Bushnell, who rejected the objective atonement
of Christ and made it simply an appeal to
man's heart, leading him to repentance, nevertheless admitted that the sinner could not get
along without the "altar forms" and ideas.
The guilty conscience requires an objective
atonement, something done for it as well as
in it.   If this be true, and it is true beyond a
doubt, wherever there is a deep sense of sin
and guilt, then it must rest upon a deep necessity of some kind.   Hence we are right in taking the Scriptures at their word when they
assert that Christ's atonement was not a mere
dramatic spectacle, a mere object lesson appeal-
ing to human hearts.   It was also based upon
a deep necessity in the law of righteousness
and in the holy character of God.

John   3:16;   Luke   19:10;   Isaiah   42:21;   Isaiah,
chapter 53;   Hebrews 1:8;   Hebrews 1:3;   Philippians
2:6, 7;   Ephesians 2:8;   Ephesians, chapter 1;   Hebrews
7:25;   Hebrews 7:26;   1 Peter 1:19;   Hebrews 1:2;   Romans 8:30;   1 Timothy 2:5, 6;   Romans 5:1ff;   Romans
3:24-26;   Hebrews 9:15.

THE HOLY SPIRIT.

The New Testament reveals to us the doctrine
of the Holy Spirit in its completed form.   His
work is a most essential and vital part of the
religion of Christ.   In the Old Testament the
Holy Spirit wrought upon the hearts of men
in manifold ways.   He was present in creation,

bringing the present cosmos out of the primeval chaos. He was present in the prophets and leaders in Israel and in many other ways his power was manifested. Not, however, until we come to the New Testament do we find the fully developed doctrine of the Holy Spirit, the third person in the Trinity.

The Holy Spirit was present everywhere in the earthly ministry of Jesus, clothing him with power for his messianic work. Through his power the body of Jesus was raised from the dead. The Spirit was given in his fullness on the day of Pentecost, to abide with the people of Christ forever. He convinces the world of sin, regenerates the heart, leads and guides Christians, making clear to them revealed truth. He sanctifies and sustains believers in trial and temptation and struggle. His mission is to glorify Christ, so that what Christ does he does, and what he does Christ does. In Paul's writings especially the doctrine of the Holy Spirit is developed most fully. The whole inner life of the believer is under his influence and subject to his power. We are commanded to grieve not, quench not, and resist not the Holy Spirit. We are sealed by the Spirit. The Spirit is the earnest of our inheritance. The fruits of the Spirit are described over against the fruits of the flesh. The Spirit teaches the apostles in their labors and in the writing of their epistles. Christ predicted that the Spirit would come thus to take his place when he left the earth and that it was expedient for him to go in order that the Holy Spirit might come.

It is a strange and very significant fact that Christians for nearly two thousand years have so generally neglected the New Testament teaching as to the Holy Spirit. The creeds of Christendom have done scant justice to the doctrine and some of the greatest of them have scarcely done more than barely mention his office work. The Philadelphia Confession of Faith used by so many Baptists and the New Hampshire Confession also quite generally used are without separate articles on the Holy Spirit, although both of them make reference to his work in connection with other doctrines. The Westminster Confession, the Presbyterian standard, is also lacking in any adequate setting forth of the work of the Holy Spirit. Of course the Holy Spirit is mentioned in these and other great creeds in the statement of the doctrine of the Trinity. But this comes far short of the full requirements of the case. The doctrine of the Holy Spirit is so interwoven and intertwined with the whole of the Old and New Testaments that it is one of the strangest oversights that Christians should have neglected it so long. One cause of this neglect is no doubt the long prevalence over wide areas of centralized and hierarchical perversions of the Christianity of the New Testament. When church government is lodged in the hands of men and Christianity becomes merged in officialism, the opportunity for the Spirit's guidance passes away. The Spirit deals directly with the heart of the individual, and the ecclesiastical official to whom is committed the function of governing does not want any other guidance for the individual apart from his own. It was found, therefore, that truly spiritual Christians must needs get away from the hierarchies as far as possible, either in the monasteries or in small heretical bodies who asserted their independence and freedom in Christ. The creeds have largely been official creeds until comparatively modern times. Hence the doctrine of the Holy Spirit has naturally been kept in the background.

Baptists have a very special interest in the doctrine of the Holy Spirit and need to reassert it with vigor. We believe in a regenerated church membership, in individualism and freedom of conscience, in the right of private judgment, and in the autonomy of the local church, in an open Bible and freedom to witness for Christ. Hence we are peculiarly dependent upon the Holy Spirit for the successful prosecution of our work.

Gen. 1:2; 2 Kings 2:9; Neh. 9:30; Ps. 104:30; Ps. 106:33; Ps. 139:7ff; Ps. 143:10; Isa. 61:1ff; Matt. 4:1; Mk. 1:10; Mk. 1:12; Luke 2:27; Luke 4:14; Jno. 1:33; Jno. 3:34; Acts, chapter 2; Rom. 1:3; Rom. 8:1; 1 Cor. 2:4; Eph. 2:18; 1 Thess. 5:19; 1 Tim. 4:1; Rev. 2:7; Rev. 22:17; John 14:16 and 26; John 15:26; Jno. 16:7.

REGENERATION.

The Holy Spirit of God regenerates the soul
of man. No human influence, no form of cul-
ture, no kind or degree of education, no law
of development works this change. The direct
action of the Holy Spirit alone accomplishes
the result. The Spirit may and does use
means, that is, the truth of God, in effecting
it. But we must not confound the agent with
the means nor the means with the agent. The
truth is made effective to regenerate only in
and through the power of the Holy Spirit.

The change wrought in regeneration is
described in the Scriptures as a "new birth",
as a "resurrection from the dead", as a being
"made alive" in Christ and in other ways
which show clearly that man is helpless, by
reason of his sinful and carnal nature, to
work this change in himself. In it he is
turned from the love of sin to the love of
holiness, from a disobedient to an obedient
life, from bondage to sin to the freedom that
is in Christ, and is translated from the kingdom of darkness into the Kingdom of light,
and led from the service of Satan into the
service of Christ.

John 1:13; 1 John 3:9; 1 John 4:7; 1 John 5:1; John
3:1-8; Tit. 3:5; 2 Cor. 5:17; 1 Pet. 1:22-25.

REPENTANCE.

Repentance is essentially a turning of the will from the life and service of sin to the life and service of holiness and of obedience to God. The word as used in the New Testament means a change of mind, but it is a word of moral significance and does not mean merely a change of opinion or judgment in the intellectual sense. Such a change may and does often take place without repentance in the New Testament meaning of the word. Here the will is directly and necessarily involved as well as the intellect and the emotions. There is a change of mind, indeed, and there is sorrow for sin. But unless sorrow and the altered judgment issue in the turning of the will from sin and its service to obedience and service of God there is no Gospel repentance. The change is wrought by the power of God through his Holy Spirit, using the word of truth to convict the sinner of sin, and to lead him to forsake it and resolve henceforth to endeavor to walk before God in a manner well pleasing in his sight.

Jer. 8:6; Jer. 20:16; Mk. 1:15; Acts 11:18; Jno. 16:8; Acts 2:37, 38; Acts 16:30, 31; Luke 18:13; Matt. 11:20, 21; Matt. 12:41; Matt. 21:19; 2 Cor. 7:10; Rev. 2:25; Rev. 16:9.

FAITH.

Saving faith includes belief and trust: belief of the facts and truths of the Gospel and trust in Jesus Christ for salvation. Faith is the grace which is the root of all other graces. When genuine it leads to a godly life. It is the condition of all God's gifts to us in Jesus Christ. It is the condition of justification and pardon, adoption and regeneration. None of these take place apart from faith. It is the action not only of the intellect but of the will and emotions as well. It brings a real knowledge of God. It is an abiding attitude of the soul and even in the life to come faith in its essential meaning of union and fellowship with God will continue. Salvation has always been conditioned on faith, not only since, but also before Christ. Abraham was saved through faith, that is to say, faith with him as with us is not a means or ground, but a condition of salvation. Our faith does not procure salvation for us, but it so relates us to Christ that he lays hold of us and saves us when we believe in him.

"But," it is said, "were not the Old Testament saints saved by works? And even now, if one should lead a perfect life, would that not be salvation by works?" The question completely overlooks the relation of faith to works. None save Jesus ever lived a perfect life. But if one should so live his good works would grow directly out of his faith. Good works are impossible in the Gospel sense without faith. The energy of God never comes into the soul in its regenerating power save through faith. In Heaven we shall be without sin and our faith will continue there. But our heavenly perfection will not be credited to us as works meriting salvation. They will be wrought in us by the power of God through our abiding union with him in Christ. Precisely thus would it have been with any pre-christian soul if such a soul had attained perfection on earth. No spiritual perfection ever has been or ever will be possible without faith, and that means without grace. Hence it is misleading to talk of salvation by works. The law was given as a schoolmaster to lead men to Christ, but it could not make alive spiritually.

Many people are troubled over the question of the order of faith and repentance. Which comes first? Clear thinking shows that the controversy on this point is a needless one. The Disciples, many of them, define faith as intellectual belief and then insist that faith must precede repentance. Many Baptists become alarmed, and to meet this view insist that repentance must precede faith. When faith is defined properly there is no occasion for any confusion of thought on the subject. Faith is more than intellectual belief, "the bare belief of the bare truth". Faith is also trust in Jesus Christ, an act of the will. Now as

to the order of repentance and faith it may
apparently be argued with equal force either
way. For example we may say: Repentance
must precede faith because saving faith is
impossible so long as we cling to sin. This is
logically cogent. Yet we may also argue thus:
Since no man can repent without the grace of
God, and since faith alone is the condition of grace in the soul, therefore faith must
precede repentance. If one is disposed to
emphasize human freedom he is likely to put
repentance first, and if he is disposed to emphasize the grace of God he will put faith first.
Thus as a mere matter of logic the case is
evenly balanced, the conclusion depending on
the starting point or major premise.

But if both are equally logical, both are
also equally illogical. There can be no interval between Gospel faith and Gospel repentance. Each is bound up in the other. When
one is completed the other is completed.
Otherwise there might be an unbelieving penitent, or an impenitent believer, either of which
ideas is contrary to the New Testament. In
strict logic regeneration precedes both faith
and repentance if we begin with the true
Gospel teaching that all is due to the grace of
God. Yet here again fact and apparent logic
do not necessarily coincide. The correct view
is that regeneration and repentance and faith
are simultaneous events in the soul's life. No
impenitent or unbelieving soul can be a regen-

erate soul, just as no penitent believer can be unregenerate. When the human side is complete so is the divine side, and *vice versa*. You may say that repentance is like opening the hand and dropping what it holds, that is sin, and that faith is opening the hand and receiving what grace brings, that is salvation. And then you may infer that just as you must open the hand and drop what it holds before you can grasp what is offered, so also repentance, or letting go, must come before faith, which grasps. This argument, however, overlooks the vital truth that grace not only places salvation in the open hand, but also relaxes the grasp of the hand on sin. The goodness of God leads to repentance. Grace not only fills the open hand. It opens the hand.

The union of God and man in the act of salvation is the actual contact of both the divine and the human personalities. And just as when you touch the table with your hand you cannot say the table touches your hand before your hand touches the table, so also you cannot affirm the priority of God's contact with man nor man's contact with God in salvation. God's grace takes the initiative but the human response in some form is simultaneous with the effectual action of God's grace in the soul and the human response is complete when the divine act is complete. When saving faith is complete so is repentance; when repentance is complete so is faith; when faith and repentance are complete so is regeneration; and when regeneration is complete so are faith and repentance.

Matt. 9:18; Mk. 1:15; Mk. 9:24; Luke 8:13; Jno. 5:44; Jno. 6:29; Jno. 9:35; Jno. 17:20; Acts 8:37; Acts 13:39; Rom. 3:22; Rom. 4:11; Eph. 1:19; Eph. 2:8; Jno. 16:8; Rom. 10:9-11; Gal. 2:16; Eph. 1:13; Rom. 3:30; Heb. 6:12; Col. 1:23; Col. 2:7; Tit. 1:13; Acts 3:16; Rom. 3:25.

JUSTIFICATION AND ADOPTION.

Justification is God's act, in and by which he declares the sinner free from condemnation. It takes place when the sinner turns from his sins and trusts in Jesus Christ and his atoning work for salvation. In justification the sinner is not actually made just or holy, but is simply given a new standing with God according to which his faith is imputed to him for righteousness since that faith terminates in and upon Jesus Christ the righteous, who is the Lamb of God that taketh away the sin of the world (Rom. 4:5, 11, 13, 22; John 1:29). Justification is to be distinguished from regeneration in that while regeneration is the change of the sinner's nature by the action of the Holy Spirit, justification is the change of the sinner's standing by a declarative act of God in which sins are remitted and the sinner is freed from condemnation. Justification again is to be distinguished from adoption in that while both are outward acts of God corresponding with the inward act of regeneration, adoption has to do with the paternal aspect of God's character and his relation to the regenerate as sons, justification is the expression of his judicial function. It is the Judge dealing with the transgressor prior to the act of the Father dealing with the son.

There is no contradiction or inconsistency between the paternal and judicial relations of God to men. Sin and trangression put the sinner outside the pale of sonship in the spiritual and evangelical sense. If sonship could exist prior to the change of the sinner's heart it would be merely a formal and unreal sonship. The Scriptures reserve the word son for the higher relation of man to God which arises when union is restored between God and man and the heart is changed by the Holy Spirit when faith in Christ takes place. God is always fatherly in his yearnings and desires toward men. He longs for all men to become filial toward him, but so long as men refuse to act toward God as sons the relationship cannot be completed. God therefore does not change his nature when men become the sons of God, but the nature of man is changed instead. This fact will help to clear up the confusion of thought in many minds as to the question of God's Fatherhood. Fatherhood and sonship are members of a reciprocal relationship which arises from similarity of moral and spiritual nature in God and man. To make God the Father of wicked men in the higher sense therefore of the spiritual relationship would put God's nature on a level with that of the sinner. Man as God's creature, made in God's image and the special object of his love, is constituted for sonship, and if sonship is defined in terms of creaturehood or original moral likeness to God all men may be called sons of God. But the Scriptures observe a wise economy in the use of the terms son and sonship by reserving it chiefly for the higher spiritual relationship, especially in the New Testament, where sonship is usually declared to be through faith in Jesus Christ. If indeed sonship in the lower and higher senses were used interchangeably it would tend to destroy the meaning of the higher, and to confuse the values and debase the coinage of the moral Kingdom.

The parable of the Prodigal Son in the fifteenth chapter of Luke shows how sin disturbs the true relations between God and man. Under the forms of fatherhood and sonship the beautiful story of man's alienation from and return to God is told. The son's sense of need was not in the first instance a filial feeling at all. It was bodily hunger. He began to be in want and would fain have eaten the husks fed to the swine. Next comes his sense of unworthiness and confession of sin. "I am no more worthy to be called thy son: make me

as one of thy hired servants", is what he says
to his father when he returns. His moral in-
stinct was quite correct. He felt, now that he
was penitent for his evil life, how far below
the plane of true sonship he had been living.
The father also recognizes this. For he says,
"My son was dead, and is alive again; he was
lost and is found". Here, then, was a son
who was not a son, and a father to whom the
son living a sinful life was dead—that is, the
son was as if he did not exist, until broken-
hearted over his sins he returns to the father.
By sin, then, the son threw away his sonship.
He still bore the original constitution derived
from his father, but all the higher elements
of his sonship were gone. I think the apparent inconsistencies in the Scriptures, where
at times there seems to be taught a universal
Fatherhood of God and sonship of man (as in
this parable), are to be explained thus. The
abnormal conditions produced by sin placing
man outside the pale of true sonship, and yet
leaving him with the moral constitution bestowed upon him when he was made in God's
image—these facts account for the language
of Scripture on the subject. God remains
paternal in his desires, his nature does not
change. The change is in men who have
wandered away from him. The inconsistency
after all, then, is not in the Scriptures, but in
man's conduct. Sometimes the Scriptures give
hints of this paternal yearning of God's heart

towards men.   Sometimes they speak of the
original and primal relation of man to God,
or refer to man as God's offspring in a general
sense as in Paul's sermon at Athens.   But we
find in the New Testament much emphasis
upon the nature of that sonship which alone
has significance for man in the highest sense,
viz., the sonship which arises through faith in
Christ, regeneration by the Spirit and moral
likeness to God, a sonship so diverse from
and so much higher than man's natural likeness to God that Paul employs the word adoption to indicate how it comes to men.

Adoption in Paul's writings then is the word
borrowed from Roman usage to express the
outward act of God corresponding with our
inner spiritual change when regeneration takes
place and we are made new creatures in moral
and spiritual qualities.

Acts 13:39; Rom. 5:9; Rom. 3:25ff; Isa. 53:11, 12;
Rom. 8:1; Rom. 5:1ff; Rom. 4:4, 5; Rom. 5:21; Rom.
6:23; Rom. 5:19; 1 Cor. 1:30, 31; 1 Tim. 4:8; Rom.
8:15; Gal. 4:5; Eph. 1:5.

SANCTIFICATION.

Sanctification is the process by which regenerate men are gradually transformed into the
image and likeness of Jesus Christ.   The word
means first to be set apart to a holy use, and
second to become actually holy.   In both
senses it applies to the Christian believer.
4.

When the Scriptures refer to sanctification as
a past act it usually is to be taken in the first
sense. The Holy Spirit in the believer carries
on the process which continues throughout the
present life. The Spirit of God employs the
word of truth, the appointments, services and
ordinances of the church, the events and experiences of our daily life and various other
means for our sanctification.

No one becomes sinless in the present life.
He may and should become more and more
complete or mature as the years pass. The
Scriptures employ the word perfect to express
the idea of symmetry and completeness in the
possession of all the parts, as well as of sinlessness. In the sense of sinlessness it never
applies to men in this life. Perfection
is the goal and ideal of our Christian
life and the most advanced, the most mature
or "perfect" Christian, Paul declares, is he who
has a sense of his own imperfections (Phil.
3:13-16).

The most saintly men and women have always been keenly alive to their shortcomings,
just as was Paul the apostle. In his later
epistles Paul seems filled as never before with
this sense of spiritual defect. He yearns to
"know" Christ and "be found in him"; he
counts not himself to have attained; he
presses "towards the mark"; he forgets the
things that are behind, etc. All this shows that
the more vividly we realize the infinite stand-

ard of holiness in our faith, the more distant
do our present attainments seem below it. A
self-complacent belief in one's own sinless "perfection", therefore, is a sure mark of spiritual
blindness. It is the same kind of mistake a
child makes who thinks he can grasp a star.
He is without appreciation of the interval between him and the star. It is this sense of
imperfection which deepens our appreciation of
the atonement of Christ and of God's love as
displayed therein. In his first epistle John declares that if we walk in the light as he is in
the light we "have fellowship one with another". Then as if overcome by the dazzling
splendor of God's light and turned back upon
his own sinfulness, he adds, "and the blood
of Jesus Christ his Son cleanseth us from all
sin" (1 John 1:7). We see then how the
sense of imperfection goes along with us
through life, deepening indeed in a real sense
as we make spiritual progress. Thus in the
Christian life we see the meaning of Paul's
paradox in his letter to the Philippians according to which the most mature or "perfect" Christian is he who most keenly realizes
his own imperfections and struggles hardest
to overcome them (Phil. 3:15). There is one
great danger we should guard against in connection with this subject of sanctification. In
opposing the "perfectionist" or "sanctification-
ist" we may easily fail to emphasize the im-
portance of growth in grace and in Christian

character. We may adopt an attitude of contentment with the ordinary conventional Christian life as against the "higher life", and this is even worse than what we oppose. We may spend our time fighting the "perfectionist" while living a worldly life ourselves. Dr. A. J. Gordon said: "It is not an edifying spectacle to see a Christian worldling hurling stones at a Christian perfectionist." We may and should meet his errors, but we should not be led thereby to adopt a low standard for ourselves.

Sanctification includes all of the Christian's relationships. Santification is social as well as individual. It is not merely an inward, it is also an outward transformation. What the Christian is in his relations to his fellowmen in business and social and civic life is the true index of the sanctifying process within. Nothing less than the highest ideal is worthy of the Christian calling. We are to aim at perfection because God our Father is perfect, and the supreme motive and incentive to the holy life is the desire to be like our Father in Heaven.

Phil. 2:12, 13; Eph. 4:11; 1 Jno. 2:29; Prov. 4:18; 1 Cor. 1:30; 1 Thess. 4:3; 2 Thess. 2:13; 1 Peter 1:2; Ex. 13:2; Ex. 28:41; Gen. 2:3; Jno. 10:36; Jno. 17:19; Acts 20:32; Rom. 15:16; 1 Cor. 1:2; Heb. 2:11; Heb. 10:10; Heb. 10:14.

THE PERSEVERANCE OF THE SAINTS.

The believer in Jesus, who has been regen‧ erated by the power of the Holy Spirit, will never utterly fall away from Christ and be lost. He is not free from temptation; he may, through neglect and failure to employ the means of grace, grieve the Holy Spirit and bring reproach upon himself and the people of God. He will, however, turn away from his sins and return to his Christian duty; he will not be content in the wayward life. It is the mark of the child of God that he cannot be happy in a life of sin. Besides this, God's care is ever over his child. God's grace ever seeks the wayward to bring them back. But just as God's loving nature and his firm purpose impel him continually to seek to win the wanderer back to the true life, so also is the renewed heart, the soul born of God's Spirit, inclined to yield to God's gracious appeals. The soul which yields no response to God's seeking love and is wholly content to live a life of world- liness and sin, thereby proclaims itself an unregenerated soul. We are not to think of God's preserving care of the redeemed, there- fore, as if it were a prevention by force and compulsion of the consequences of a sinful life. The responsive perseverance of the Christian is as essential a part of the process as God's preserving grace. This is the explanation of many New Testament passages which seem to imply that all depends on the act of the believer and not on the grace of God. The grace of God is effective only when it produces the necessary response. The possibility of a fall is quite a real one apart from the grace of God. In vain also is the grace of God apart from the response of our will. The New Testament writers do not hesitate, therefore, to state boldly and strongly both facts, in order that God's grace may become effective, through warning and exhortation, in the turning of the wayward will back again to the path of duty. God does not lift his children into Heaven against their wills. The whole of the machinery or system of grace, therefore, is designed to make them willing. Thus do they persevere while at the same time they are preserved. Here again much confusion of thought grows out of the ordinary way of thinking of God's grace as if it were a physical or mechanical force, like a rope tied around a Christian to keep him from drowning, or a wall built to prevent him from falling over a precipice. The New Testament does not represent it that way at all. It has many terrible warnings against apostasy—not indeed to teach apostasy but to prevent it. These passages are bewildering to the Christian who thinks of God's preserving care as an outward wall compelling us to keep away from the precipice. God preserves us by inclining us to persevere.

A mother sent her four-year-old boy on an errand across a busy city street full of dangers of all kinds. A friend expressed surprise. The mother said the child had been taught to look carefully up and down before venturing across and she had no fear. This was training. The other would no doubt have seized her child by the hand and towed him across. God's method is not to tow us but to train us. Grace does not compel, it inclines us. The New Testament emphasizes training as against towing. If we keep this in mind we will understand many otherwise difficult passages.

Jno. 8:31; 1 Jno. 2:19, 27, 28; 1 Jno. 3:9; 1 Jno. 5:18; Rom. 8:28, 29; Phil. 1:6; Phil. 2:12, 13; 1 Jno. 4:4; Jno. 10:26-29.

THE KINGDOM OF GOD.

The eternal purpose of God in the revelation of his will to man in the incarnation and work of Christ was the establishment of his Kingdom on earth. We can here give only a very condensed outline of the meaning of the Kingdom of God, or the Kingdom of Heaven, both of which forms of expression are found in the New Testament. In the Old Testament all created things are represented as belonging to God's Kingdom. As Creator he is Lord of all things, inanimate as well as animate, suns and stars as well as animals and men and angels. He establishes, however, a Kingdom among men in the call of Abraham and in the covenant with Israel as a nation. That Kingdom passes through various stages, in the patriarchal, Mosaic, kingly and prophetic periods in the history of Israel. In none of these is the idea of the Kingdom perfectly realized. The incarnation of Jesus Christ continued God's work of revelation. The preaching of Jesus had as its central truth the Kingdom of God. He called men to repentance because the Kingdom of God "is at hand". There are various phases of meaning found in the word as it is employed in the New Testament. It means primarily the reign or rule or dominion of God in the human heart and life, but everywhere the Kingdom in the larger and wider sense of God's rule in the universe is taken for granted. In the New Testament the Kingdom of God is an inward and outward power. It is a present and a future reality. Sin 'has disturbed God's rule on earth and grace has come in the person of Christ and through his atoning work to restore it. In the New Testament especially is the Kingdom of God a new principle of redemption in the heart changing men into the moral and spiritual character required by God's will. Righteousness in all its forms is the aim and end of the Kingdom of God. The Gospel is God's appointed means for the realization of the righteousness of the Kingdom. This Kingdom of God is not to be identified with any

outward ecclesiastical or civil form of government. In one of its phases it is practically
identical with the spiritual or universal church.
But it never coincides exactly with any outward
form of ecclesiastical or civil government.

The local church is in harmony, or is meant
to be in harmony, with the principles of the
Kingdom. In a real sense it reproduces, or lo-
calizes, and perpetuates the Kingdom of God
on earth. Its doctrines and polity must conform to the teachings and to the essential nature of the Kingdom. The Kingdom recedes
somewhat into the background after we leave
the gospels and enter the epistles. The church
is more prominent in the epistles. Nevertheless the Kingdom still appears in the teaching
of the epistles. Its inner nature is described
and its future triumph is clearly indicated.
Christ is King in the Kingdom, both in the
gospels and in the epistles, and he will come
at last and as its King he will judge the world
and bestow upon men their final awards. The
Kingdom thus passes from the earthly to the
heavenly and eternal stage. When Christ's
mediatorial work is consummated he delivers
up the Kingdom to God the Father. His atoning death was necessary to the realization of
the ends of the Kingdom and a great and in-
dispensable step was taken when the Spirit was
given at Pentecost. The duty of Christ's people is to labor for the coming of God's King-

dom on earth, even as he taught us in the Lord's prayer.

Gen. 2:4ff; Ps. 47:7; Ps. 103:19ff; Ps. 104:4ff; Ps. 119:89ff; Is. 1:2, 3; Is. 43:21; Ex. 19:3-6; Jer. 31:31ff; Ezek. 17:22ff; Matt. 11:10ff; Matt. 3:5, 6; Mk. 1:5; Luke 3:7ff; Jno. 1:19-27; Matt. 13:41; 16:28; 20:21; 25:34; Mk. 1:15; Luke 7:50; 13:3-5; Jno. 18:37; Matt. 5:13-16; 7:21; 7:22; 10:23; 13:41; Luke 12:8; Matt. 13:40; 19:28; Acts 8:12; 14:22; 19:8; 1 Cor. 15:24ff; Eph. 5:5; Col. 1:13; Rev. 1:6; 3:21; 5:10; 11:16, 17; 20:1-8.

THE SECOND COMING OF CHRIST.

The Scriptures teach that Christ will return in person to this earth. The time of his return is not revealed. The Scriptures do not seem to warrant the belief that a state of perfect piety will exist on earth when Christ returns. Christians are commanded to expect the coming of the Lord always. New Testament Christians did this. There was no explicit teaching that Christ was to come in the New Testament age, but Christians were constantly expecting his return. This expectation should not tempt us to do slovenly or superficial work, or neglect our duty. It should rather make us conscientious and faithful in the highest degree. The New Testament reveals no program of events which is to follow the return of Christ. The event itself was the center of the expectation. He may come tomorrow. He may not come in ten thousand years.

Matt. 24:27; Matt 25:34f; Mk. 13:3-37; Luke 21:5ff; Acts 1:11; 1 Thess. 5:1-3; 2 Thess. 2:1-12.

THE RESURRECTION.

At death the bodies of all return to dust. There is to be a resurrection both of the just and the unjust. Little is taught in Scripture regarding the resurrection of the wicked apart from the fact itself. In the fifteenth chapter of First Corinthians, however, Paul gives a very glorious account of the resurrection of the dead in Christ. Their resurrection bodies are to be free from all sin and infirmity and perfectly fitted for the glorified spirit. At death the spirits of believers go to Christ. At the resurrection body and spirit are reunited and glorified and enter fully upon the eternal reward in Christ.

Matt. 22:30; Luke 14:14; John 5:29; Acts 1:22; Acts 4:2; Acts 24:15; Rom. 6:5; 1 Cor. ch. 15; Phil. 3:10; 2 Tim. 2:18; Rev. 20:6.

THE JUDGMENT.

God has appointed a day wherein he will judge the world by Jesus Christ. All men are to appear before the judgment seat of Christ. The word judgment means discrimination. At the judgment men are to be discriminated or separated according to moral character. The Scripture teaching as to the judgment day does not mean that the final destiny of men remains uncertain until that judgment takes place, as if God were ignorant as to their condition until he made an investigation. The judgment is rather the formal declaration of conditions which had previously existed. It is the manifestation or exhibition of the righteousness and the love, along with other attributes of God. The principle of judgment is in operation in the earthly life of men in a certain sense. The moral law operates always and everywhere. The final judgment, however, is the necessary culmination of these temporal judgments. God's ways will then be vindicated to men, and the justice of all his dealings with them be made plain. Men will then know and feel the justice of all God's ways. Even wicked men, in the illumination of that judgment, will recognize the justice of God's decree concerning them.

The Scriptures declare that the righteous do not come into judgment (John 3:18 and 5:24). This, however, does not mean that they will be absent when the great assize shall take place. For Paul declares explicitly that we shall all be made manifest before the judgment seat of Christ (2 Cor. 5:10). We need only to remember that the word judgment means to discriminate, in order to harmonize these apparently contradictory Scriptures. The discrimination of judgment will divide men into two classes. One class will be condemned, the other approved. The word judgment is often used to indicate the condemnatory side of the process. To be judged means, in that case, to be condemned. This is what John means when he asserts that believers shall not come into judgment. Not the condemnatory but the approbatory aspect of judgment will befall believers. They shall not come into condemnation, although they, too, shall stand before the judgment seat of Christ.

Judgment is to be according to works. Unbelief on the part of sinners leads to evil works; faith on the part of Christians leads to good works. Works in both cases are the outward expression of a deeper condition, the attitude of faith or of unbelief. The fundamental principle which fixes a man's place in the scale of moral worth is that of faith and unbelief. Since the judgment does not fix or determine destiny, but simply declares or exhibits it, it is based on the outward expression of the soul's deeper attitude of unbelief and of faith. As works are the outward sign of the inward state, and as judgment likewise is the manifestation or outward sign of the inward state, it is entirely fitting that judgment should proceed on the principle of works.

Matt. 25:32ff; Matt. 12:36; Acts 17:31; Jno. 5:22, 27; Rom. 9:22, 23; Mk. 9:48; 2 Thess. 1:5-7; Mk. 13:35, 37; Luke 12:35-40; Rev. 22:20; Matt. 13:49; Rom. 3:5, 6; Rev. 20:11-15.

THE CHURCH.

There are two chief senses in which the word church is used in the New Testament. In a number of passages it refers to all believers, whether they are thought of as existing on earth, or on earth and in Heaven at any particular time, or as the total assembly of the redeemed in the life to come. Some take the New Testament teaching as to the universal church in the last sense alone, that is, they assert that the universal church has no existence at present on earth in any sense, but that in the life to come the local church will cease to be and the universal church will come into existence. There are passages, however, which forbid this view. For example, in Ephesians 5:25-27 we read: "Husbands, love your wives, even as Christ also loved the church, and gave himself up for it; that he might sanctify it, having cleansed it by the washing of water with the word, that he might present the church to himself a glorious church, not having spot or wrinkle or any such thing; but that it should be holy and without blemish." In this passage the church is viewed as existing in time and in eternity and the continuity of the church which exists in time with that which exists in eternity is made indisputably clear. In time it is a church with spots and wrinkles; in eternity it is without spot or wrinkle. In time it needed cleansing by the washing of water, that is, it was an impure church not yet free from sin. In eternity this same church stands before Christ holy and without blemish. Now if the church here existing in time refers to the local church, then it means the same when it becomes holy and without blemish in eternity, and we have the local church with pastors, deacons and ordinances carried over into eternity. I know of no one who holds this view. The "generic" use of the word church is incompatible with Paul's meaning here. The "generic" sense in which Paul sometimes employs the word refers to the church as an institution without referring to any particular church. Yet in, this usage the local church is the institution referred to, which, as we have seen, cannot be described in the language of the passage we are dealing with.

Since, then, Paul clearly means the same thing in both parts of the sentence, his language can only refer to the totality of believers both in time and in eternity. The universal church is not an outward organization at all nor can it be made co-extensive with ecclesiastical bodies scattered over the earth made up of organized parts or branches. It has no earthly ecclesiastical functions or powers. Yet it is most real in that it includes all true believers in Jesus Christ. Faith in Jesus Christ indeed is the spiritual reality at the basis of the life of all local churches. If it be insig-

nificant or valueless or unreal because it is
spiritual, then that same quality is equally
insignificant and valueless in the local church.
The visible and tangible in the Christian religion is valueless without the invisible and
spiritual. The universal church is as real as
the Kingdom of God; indeed, it is practically
identical with it. We are not warranted, however, in refusing to employ the word church
in this general sense. The New Testament
by its own very clear usage gives us most ample
warrant for using the word church in the universal sense as defined in the preceding
remarks.

The great majority of the New Testament
passages use the word church to indicate a
local body composed of believers in Jesus Christ
who are associated together for the cultivation
of the Christian life, the maintenance of the
ordinances and discipline, and for the propa-
gation of the Gospel. Jesus Christ is Lord
of the church. It exists in obedience to his
command, and has no mission on earth save
the carrying out of his will. It must not form
alliances of any kind with the state so that
it surrenders any of its own functions or assumes any of the functions of civil government.
Its government is democratic and autonomous.
Each church is free and independent. No
church or group of churches has any authority
over any other church. Co-operation in Christian work, however, is one of the highest duties

and privileges of the churches of Jesus Christ.
Yet in so doing they do not form or consti-
tute an ecclesiasticism with functions and
powers to be authoritatively exercised over the
local bodies. The voluntary principle is the
heart of the Scripture teaching as to the individual and as to local churches. All souls
are entitled to equal privileges in the church,
just as all churches are entitled to equal privileges in the Kingdom of God. The individual precedes the group logically as well
as in order of time, and the organization
and government of the local church pro-
ceeds on the principle of the voluntary
association of free individuals in obedience
to Christ and for purposes set forth by
him. Church discipline is simply the group
protecting itself against the individual. The
church has no power of coercion in the religious life of the individual. The individual
stands or falls to his own Master, and is
judged only by him. The right of the church,
however, to protect itself against the disorderly
individual is an unalienable right in Christ.
The objection sometimes made against church
discipline on the score that it is unwarranted
coercion overlooks this fact.

Here we may point out the relation of local
Baptist churches to general Baptist bodies,
missionary, educational, etc. The latter are not
composed of churches but of individuals.
Churches may use them or not use them, co-

5

operate with them or refuse to co-operate with them. In all such co-operation or refusal to co-operate, however, the church neither assumes authority over the general body, nor submits to the authority of that body. The relation is voluntary on both sides. The church does not create nor is it created by the general body. Where a church is out of harmony with a general body it cannot legislate the general body into harmony with itself but it can withdraw if necessary without the consent of the general body. A general body has no power to retain an unwilling church in co-operative relations with it. There is no conflict of jurisdiction between a church and a general body where messengers come from churches into meetings of general bodies. As members of the general body they vote and act as individual freemen in Christ. They may act under the influences of the known wishes of their churches in measures which are considered in the general body. This, however, is not ecclesiastical compulsion but spiritual influence. General bodies are themselves autonomous. No Baptist general body has authority over another. They exist in a graded series but this does not imply legislative or judicial authority. It is for convenience and efficiency. Each body is self determining as to constitution and by laws, aims and purposes, territorial limits and methods. There are certain necessities which arise out of these principles of

Baptist organization. 1. The necessity for clear thinking in order to avoid confusion in ideals and collision in the practical work of the Kingdom. 2. The necessity for well defined limits of function and aim in the general body to avoid the assumption of church functions. 3. The necessity for courtesy and respect as between Baptist general bodies.

The officers of the church are bishops or elders and deacons. The New Testament employs the word bishop and elder to designate the same officer, these terms being descriptive of functions and not of separate officials. The bishop or elder is an officer of the local church, not of any group of churches with general jurisdiction. His authority is that of influence and leadership rather than official. He is called of the Holy Spirit to the work and is set apart by ordination for the discharge of special functions and has no authority to lord it over God's heritage. And yet as leader and guide the church owes to him its loyalty and support. His task is particularly that of spiritual leadership, while the deacons are charged rather with the temporal affairs of the church.

The ordinances of a church are baptism and the Lord's Supper. These two set forth in a very beautiful and comprehensive way the fundamental truths of the Gospel. They are not sacraments but ordinances; they do not confer or communicate or impart grace in and of themselves. They are outward symbols which signify very profound truths and these truths have vital power in the Christian life when duly apprehended or spiritually discerned by the recipient when the ordinances are administered. There is no Scripture warrant whatever for any increase in the number of the ordinances from two to seven or any other number. The Roman Catholic Church is wholly wrong in this matter and the multiplication of sacraments is a great evil in that body.

Matt. 16:18; Matt. 18:17; Acts 2:47; Acts 8:1; Acts 14:23; Rom. 16:5; 1 Cor. 14:4, 5, 23; Eph. 1:22; Eph. 3:10; Eph. 5:24-32; Col. 1:18; Heb. 12:23.

BAPTISM.

Baptism is an ordinance of Jesus Christ established for perpetual observance by his people. Every believer or regenerate person is under obligation to submit to this ordinance of Jesus Christ. Baptism is the immersion in water of the believer in the name of the Father, and of the Son, and of the Holy Spirit. The truths symbolized in baptism are the following: 1. Remission of sins. 2. Fellowship or union with Christ in his death and resurrection. The form of baptism strikingly symbolizes death, burial and resurrection. 3. Cleansing from all unrighteousness and consecration to the service of God, a complete self-surrender to the service of the Kingdom of God and resolve to walk in newness of life. Baptism is a prerequisite to church fellowship, and to participation in the Lord's Supper. Immersion is essential to Christian baptism. Other forms destroy the meaning of the ordinance. The consensus of the scholarship of all denominations declares that immersion only is baptism. The Greek word to which our word baptism corresponds can only mean immersion.

Baptism does not regenerate. It is to be administered to those who have previously been regenerated by the Spirit of God. Baptism does not secure remission of sins save in a symbolic way. The previously forgiven person is the only proper subject for baptism. Baptism is simply the outward symbol of what has already taken place within the subject. Baptism confers no spiritual but only a symbolic remission of sins. Baptism "for remission of sins" (Acts 2:38) has reference only to the symbolic remission set forth by the act. Forgiveness, or remission, is inherently a divine act and to make it a function of baptism is to ascribe a divine function to an outward ordinance. Moreover, if baptism actually conferred remission of sins, it would have to be repeated after each sin, whereas baptism is administered once only to each believer.

Matt. 3:7ff; Matt. 21:25; Mk. 1:4; Rom. 6:4; Eph. 4:5; Col. 2:12; 1 Peter 3:21; Mk. 1:9ff; Acts 2:38; Acts 2:41; Acts 8:38; Acts 18:8; Gal. 3:27.

THE LORD'S SUPPER.

The Lord's Supper is an ordinance of Christ's church wherein the elements are bread and wine. The bread symbolizes the body of Christ given for the salvation of men and the wine symbolizes his blood shed for the remission of sins. The participants of this ordinance are those who have been baptized upon a profession of their faith, and who walk in an orderly manner as members of a church of Christ.

The following errors have been associated with the Lord's Supper and are to be rejected wholly:

(a) The claim that in it there is a repetition of the sacrifice of Jesus for the sins of the world, as in the Roman Catholic sacrifice of the mass.

(b) The claim that the bread and wine are the real body and blood of Christ, as in the false doctrine of transubstantiation.

(c) The denial of the cup to the people and in any way unduly exalting or worshiping the bread and wine of the ordinance.

All the above are fatal errors and wholly opposed to the real meaning of the New Testament. Like baptism, the Lord's Supper is a symbolic ordinance. It commemorates Christ's death; it declares or sets forth that death when observed; and it is prophetic of Christ's return to his people at the end of the Gospel age. In all these respects, however, it is not a sacrament but simply an ordinance whose value is in the truth symbolized rather than in its power to impart grace. To observe the ordinance properly is to discern the truth symbolized in it. The unworthy observance of the ordinance consists in the failure to discern spiritually the body and blood of Christ.

Acts 2:41, 42; 1 Cor. 11:26ff; Matt. 26:26-29; Mk. 14: 22-25; Luke 22:14-23.

THE LORD'S DAY.

The Lord's day is a Christian institution for regular observance. Works of necessity and mercy may be performed on the Lord's day, but it should be observed in resting from ordinary employments and in exercises of worship and spiritual devotion.

The first day of the week came to be observed by Christians instead of the seventh, since this seems to have been the custom of the Christians of the New Testament. Thus it perpetuates the Old Testament principle of observing one day in seven, while giving it a Christian significance by connecting it with the resurrection of Christ which occurred on the first day of the week.

The Lord's day as a civil is not to be confounded with it as a religious institution. The state may enact laws for the observance of one day in seven in a secular way without giving to them any religious significance in the wider sense. Like laws against stealing or murder, the state may enact such laws. But the state has no authority to compel men to engage in worship or other religious activities on Sunday. Religion is voluntary and religious liberty is opposed to any legal compulsion whatsoever in religious matters. This distinction needs to be made clear. Christians sometimes imagine that the state ought to make men observe the Sabbath religiously; while non-christians sometimes imagine that the legal prohibitions contained in Sunday laws are unwarranted intrusions of the state into their religious life. Both are wrong. The state cannot prescribe what man shall do on Sunday. It can only enact what they shall not do. These negative enactments are not religious but civil in character, called for by public policy and the general welfare. As we shall see in the next article the state is without any religious function whatsoever.

Gen. 2:3; Col. 2:16, 17; Mk. 2:27; 1 Cor. 16:1, 2; Acts 20:7; Ex. 20:8; Rev. 1:10; Isa. 58:13, 14; Heb. 10:24, 25; Heb. 4:3-11.

LIBERTY OF CONSCIENCE.

A free church in a free state is a New Testament principle which has found full expression only in modern times and in the Western hemisphere. It is familiar to us in America and needs but brief treatment here. The great principle underlying religious liberty is this: God alone is Lord of the conscience. To him men must give account and only to him. The principle which corresponds with this on the side of the state is that civil magistrates are ordained of God. For its own ends the state is sovereign. But those ends do not include the religious life of the individual at all. Hence the civil and religious life of man belong to different spheres entirely. The right of every soul to direct access to God is an inalienable right, with which the state must not interfere.

(Note. The author has given much more extended discussion to the subject of this section in his work entitled "The Axioms of Religion".)

Rom. 13:1-7; Matt. 22:21; Acts 5:29; Matt. 10:28, Matt. 23:10; Rom. 14:4; Jno. 4:23, 24.

MISSIONS.

The duty of every Christian man and the duty of every church of Christ is to seek to extend the Gospel to the ends of the earth. No Christian and no church is exempt from this obligation. By personal effort, by witnessing for Christ, by gifts of money, by prayer, by co-operation with missionary boards and conventions, by going in person to do missionary work in the community and state, and nation, and the world—all these are forms of

statement of the missionary obligation. This
obligation rests upon the things implied in
our own regenerate life—since the new birth
means the birth of love for others needing salvation; it rests upon the express command of
Christ given in the great commission; it rests
upon a spiritual necessity of our renewed life
which remains dwarfed and stunted without
missionary activity; it rests upon God's eternal
purpose which is being wrought out in time,
and which incorporates in itself the co-operation of all the redeemed along with all the
necessary agencies; it rests upon the incarnation and atonement of Christ—since these,
apart from missions, cannot be adequately explained.

Matt. 28:18-20; **Mk.** 16:15-17; Luke 24:47-49; **Acts**
1:6-8.

EDUCATION.

It is unusual to refer to education as a doctrine. Yet there is ample warrant in the New
Testament for such reference. In the great
commission Jesus couples the duty of teaching
with the duty of preaching. The teaching and
preaching therein enjoined are co-ordinate and
equal parts of the great task of Christ's people.
The academy, the college, the university, indeed, all forms of organization for teaching
the truth, all institutions for the diffusion of
knowledge are the direct and logical outcome

of the work of evangelization. The Christian life involves a particular view of the world and of God as its providential Ruler and Christianity in its doctrine of regeneration lays the foundation for education.

Baptists in a very special sense are under obligation to foster Christian education. Some of the reasons are as follows: First, the Baptist emphasis on regeneration. A regenerate church membership is a cardinal Baptist doctrine. The regenerate life is the unfolding or growing life in which all the powers of man are alive and demand satisfaction. Education alone can meet all these demands. Again, the non-sacramental character of the Baptist view of the ordinances implies intelligence in the participant. The ordinances do not magically convey grace. Only as we clearly perceive the meaning of baptism and the Lord's Supper do we observe them aright. This is the Baptist view. Clearly then intelligence is required for their proper observance. The Baptist view of church government, that is, the equality of believers and local self-government in the churches, requires education. Self-government requires intelligence. Baptists believe not in episcopal authority in the ministry but spiritual leadership. An educated ministry is essential therefore to their success in the world. The right of private judgment in interpreting the Scriptures is another fundamental Baptist belief. This necessitates intelligence. Again volun-

tary co-operation in missionary and other
forms of activity in the Kingdom of God is our
only Baptist method of working together for
these great ends. Hence, we require intelligence and breadth of view, the ability to see
things in their larger relations and to adapt
means to ends, for the bringing in of the Kingdom of God. All this makes imperative the
education of our people as widely as possible.

Christian education is not necessarily in conflict with education by the state. Indeed they
mutually supplement each other. The public
school system is necessary, but Christian ideals
and the Christian type of civilization are dependent upon education under Christian au-
spices. Other things being equal, therefore,
the denomination of Christians which most
widely and most thoroughly promotes education will most deeply impress the world. At
home and abroad there comes to Baptists of
our times an imperative call to reinforce
existing schools and to establish new ones
wherever they are needed.

Deut. 4:5ff; Ps. 119; Is. 54:13; Jno. 8:2; Matt. 28:20;
Acts 15:35; 18:11; 28:31; Rom. 12:7; Col. 1:28; Gal.
6:6; Is. 9:15; 1 Jno. 2:27; Luke 23:5.

SOCIAL SERVICE.

Baptists believe in every form of righteousness: Personal righteousness or right living in
individual conduct; domestic righteousness or

right living in the home; civic righteousness or right living in the state; social righteousness or right living in society; commercial righteousness or right living in business. This demand for righteousness in all spheres is the direct result of the doctrine of regeneration. The new birth affects the whole person in all relationships. No Baptist, therefore, can be indifferent to movements for the improvement or purification of life anywhere.

The Gospel is adequate for the solution of all social problems. Patience and perseverance and intelligence of a high order, however, are required to apply the principles of righteousness to all life's relationships. The church, as such, cannot enact laws, or become the organ of social reform save indirectly. Yet the pulpit should expound the principles of right living in all spheres, and members of our churches should stand for all forms of righteousness not only in their own personal life but in public life as well.

Ezek. 8:5ff; Ezek. 18:28ff; Hosea, chs. 4 and 5; Amos, chs. 3 and 4; Matt., chs. 5 to 7; Rom., chs. 12 to 16; Epistle of James.

HEAVEN AND HELL.

According to Christian teaching Heaven is both a place and a state. The emphasis in the New Testament is everywhere upon the character which fits a man for Heaven rather than the exact locality or precise teaching as to the activities of Heaven. The place and the environment fit the character but the character is more determinative of the environment than environment is of character.

In Heaven we persist in our individual lives. Christianity everywhere emphasizes the value of personality and individuality. The Christian Heaven is far removed from the Buddhist or Brahman reabsorption in the infinite or Nirvana. As personality survives in the life to come, of course earthly experiences and earthly knowledge leave their permanent impress upon us. Earthly ties and what they meant to us are a part of ourselves. There would be little or nothing of any one of us left if the life on earth and our earthly relationships were blotted out in Heaven. Memory survives along with will and intellect. Our whole earthly life and experience enter into the final result in character, although of course all is transfigured, purified and glorified. The question often asked whether Christians will know each other in Heaven, really answers itself upon slight reflection apart from the hints which Scripture gives. We could scarcely remain ourselves without such recognition. The change which comes at death is not a change of moral character or of individuality. If you shoot an arrow across a river it is the same arrow on the other side as on this. If you put a diamond in a casket and carry it into the next room it is the same dia-

mond when you reopen the casket and take it
out. So also with us in death. The soul, the
individuality, the character, is the arrow. When
it is shot across the stream of death it abides
the same. Its surroundings are changed but it
remains fundamentally what it was. This life
gives shape to the jewel of the soul, cuts its
angles and facets, as it were; the next life may
brighten it and perfect its shape, but it remains
essentially the same.

In the New Testament Heaven is represented to us in symbols or figures of speech for
the most part and the descriptions of it are in
large measure negative rather than positive.
We gather, however, that there are at least
three elements of bliss in the New Testament
picture of Heaven. First, Heaven is relief;
relief from sin, from care, from loss, from sorrow, from laborious and exhausting toil, relief
in short from all the things which blight and
curse our life on earth. Secondly, Heaven is
reward. In the early chapters of the Revelation
the rewards of Heaven are set forth under nu-
merous forms which are very suggestive of individuality and variety in their bestowment.
The pillar in the temple of God suggests sta-
bility; the right to enter into the gates of the
city suggests privilege; the white robe suggests
purity; the white stone suggests intimacy of
personal relation with Christ; that God shall
wipe away all tears from our eyes is an exqui-
sitely tender and sublime declaration of com-

fort for the sorrowing. In the third place, Heaven is realization. No doubt many lives which are broken and disappointed will find fruition and self-realization in the life to come. Heaven is represented as a place of intense activity, since the redeemed serve God day and night in his temple. Heaven as a place of eternal inactivity would be of little value and very unattractive. The sluggard is the last man who should dream of Heaven as the fulfillment of his ideal. The rest of Heaven does not mean cessation from work, but from toilsome and exhausting work. We are made for action in body and brain alike. Inaction therefore would be death. Heaven as realization, then, means joyous activity without exhaustion in a perfect environment, and in a perfectly congenial society. It means eternal growth towards God and his infinitude, eternal achievement and a joy corresponding.

The awards of the day of judgment will be final. The wicked shall go away into endless punishment, the righteous into eternal life. The same word applies to the duration of the state of both classes. That word is not merely qualitative as if it described only the nature and not the duration of the awards of the two classes. It also means duration, that is, endlessness. So far as the Scriptures teach we must hold to the endlessness of the state of the wicked as well as the righteous and the Scriptures are very explicit on the point.

Passages which have been cited to prove that
the wicked may have a second probation and
be fully restored, are none of them conclusive,
and all must be understood in the light of
those passages which admit of no doubt whatsoever.

It is sometimes urged that it is unfair to in-
flict infinite punishment for a finite sin. This
objection overlooks the fact that the punishment will continue no longer than the sin.
Sinners confirmed in sin will sin forever. The
punishment will simply keep pace with the sin.

It is a mistake to make the problem and the
mystery of eternal punishment turn wholly on
the question of God's love. It turns equally
on the question of human freedom and man's
choice of evil. Men would revolt in the depth
of their souls and rebel with all their power if
God were to use coercion in dealing with us in
the sense of forcing our wills. This he will not
do because he has endowed us with freedom.
And yet the demand that all men be finally
saved as a means of vindicating God's government is equivalent to a demand that God shall
use coercion and compel the lost to repent.
Freedom is God's gift to man which lifts him
above the brutes and makes him like God.
Yet it is an endowment with fearful alterna-
tives of choice. We should think of this when
we are tempted to arraign God's government
for the existence of an endless hell. Hell is
the monumental expression of the abuse of

6

human freedom. This is the key to its meaning. This alone explains it.

Eph. 1:3-20; 3:10; 2 Tim. 4:18; Heb. 11:16; Matt. 5:22-29; 10:28; 11:23; 18:9; Luke 16:23; 2 Peter 4:1; Matt. 19:29; Luke 18:30; Mk. 3:29; Matt. 25:40ff; Rev., chs. 2 and 3; 14:10, 11; Rev., chs. 20, 21, 22, 23.

THE NEW HAMPSHIRE DECLARATION OF FAITH.

Two notable Confessions of Faith have found acceptance among Baptists in America, the Philadelphia Confession, which was promulgated by the Philadelphia Baptist Association, and the New Hampshire "Declaration" promulgated by the State Convention of New Hampshire. The former is a lengthy document. When published in Charleston, S. C., 1813, with the addition of a "Summary of Church Discipline" and "The Baptist Catechism", it contained three hundred and three pages. No record is had of the first publication of this Confession, but in 1742 a new edition was officially ordered printed. It bears the imprimatur of Benjamin Franklin.

Prof. W. J. McGlothlin, D.D., Ph.D., says in his "Baptist Confessions of Faith", page 298:

"Many churches and other associations, both North and South, adopted this Confession. In recent years it has been losing ground, especially in the North, but it is still widely used, and in the South is probably the most influential of all Confessions."

This Confession is strongly Calvinistic, and it is an exact reproduction of the Assembly Confession, London, 1689, with the addition of two articles, one on Singing Psalms and the other on Laying on of Hands, both of which are commended.

The New Hampshire Declaration, as will be seen, came much later and is very much shorter. It was incorporated by Dr. J. M. Pendleton, 1867, in his "Church Manual"; and by Dr. E. T. Hiscox, 1890, in his "Standard Manual". Recently it has been adopted by the Landmark Convention and as well by the Southwestern Baptist Theological Seminary, the latter making one change which causes "visible" church to read "particular" church.

Dr. J. Newton Brown, 1853, editorial secretary of the American Baptist Publication Society, did more than anyone else to bring this Declaration to its present form. On his own authority he revised it and added two articles. The changes made are enclosed in brackets. The two new articles are numbers VIII. and X. This Declaration has become almost the sole Confession used in the North, East and West, where Calvinism has become most modified by Arminianism. The word "Declaration" is used for this Confession because the New Hampshire Baptists expressly so decided it should be called. Those who may wish for a more extended dis-

cussion of Baptist Confessions are referred to
Prof. McGlothlin's book to which we have referred.

The New Hampshire Declaration is as follows:

I. OF THE SCRIPTURES.

We believe [that] the Holy Bible was written by men divinely inspired, and is a perfect
treasure of heavenly instruction; that it has
God for its author, salvation for its end, the
truth, without any mixture of error, for its
matter; that it reveals the principles by which
God will judge us; and therefore is, and shall
remain to the end of the world, the true center
of Christian union, and the supreme standard
by which all human conduct, creeds, and opin-
ions should be tried.

II. OF THE TRUE GOD.

[We believe] That there is one, and only
one, living and true God, [an infinite, intelligent Spirit,] whose name is Jehovah, the
Maker and Supreme Ruler of Heaven and
earth; inexpressibly glorious in holiness; [and]
worthy of all possible honor, confidence and
love; revealed under the personal and relative
distinctions of the Father, the Son, and the
Holy Spirit; equal in every divine perfection,
and executing distinct but harmonious offices
in the great work of redemption.

III. OF THE FALL OF MAN.

[We believe] That man was created in a state of holiness, under the law of his Maker; but by voluntary transgression fell from that holy and happy state; in consequence of which all mankind are now sinners, not by constraint but choice, being by nature utterly void of that holiness required by the law of God, wholly given to the gratification of the world, of Satan and of their own sinful passions, therefore under just condemnation to eternal ruin, without defense or excuse.

IV. OF THE WAY OF SALVATION.

[We believe] That the salvation of sinners is wholly of grace; through the Mediatorial Offices of the Son of God, who [by the appointment of the Father, freely] took upon him our nature, yet without sin; honored the [divine] law by his personal obedience, and made atonement for our sins by his death; being risen from the dead he is now enthroned in Heaven; and uniting in his wonderful person the tenderest sympathies with divine perfections, [he] is every way qualified to be a suitable, a compassionate and an all-sufficient Savior.

V. OF JUSTIFICATION.

[We believe] That the great Gospel blessing which Christ of his fullness bestows on such as believe in him, is justification; that justification consists in the pardon of sin and the promise of eternal life, on principles of righteousness; that it is bestowed not in consideration of any works of righteousness which we have done, but solely through his own redemption and righteousness, [by virtue of which faith his perfect righteousness is freely imputed to us of God;] that it brings us into a state of most blessed peace and favor with God, and secures every other blessing needful for time and eternity.

VI. OF THE FREENESS OF SALVATION.

[We believe] That the blessings of salvation are made free to all by the Gospel; that it is the immediate duty of all to accept them by a cordial, [penitent,] and obedient faith; and that nothing prevents the salvation of the greatest sinner on earth except his own [inherent depravity and] voluntary refusal to submit to the Lord Jesus Christ, which refusal will subject him to an aggravated condemnation.

VII. OF GRACE IN REGENERATION.

[We believe] that in order to be saved, we must be regenerated or born again; that regeneration consists in giving a holy disposition to the mind; and is effected in a manner above our comprehension or calculation, by the power of the Holy Spirit, [in connection with divine truth,] so as to secure our voluntary obedience to the Gospel; and that its proper evidence is found in the holy fruit which we bring forth to the glory of God.

VIII. OF REPENTANCE AND FAITH.

[This article added in 1853.]

We believe that Repentance and Faith are sacred duties, and also inseparable graces, wrought in our souls by the regenerating Spirit of God; whereby being deeply convinced of our guilt, danger, and helplessness, and of the way of Salvation by Christ, we turn to God with unfeigned contrition, confession, and supplication for mercy; at the same time heartily receiving the Lord Jesus Christ as our Prophet, Priest and King, and relying on him alone as the only and all-sufficient Savior.

IX. OF GOD'S PURPOSE OF GRACE.

[We believe] That Election is the gracious purpose of God, according to which he [graciously] regenerates, sanctifies, and saves sinners; that being perfectly consistent with the free agency of man, it comprehends all the means in connection with the end; that it is a most glorious display of God's sovereign goodness, being infinitely [free,] wise, holy, and unchangeable; that it utterly excludes boasting, and promotes humility, [love,] prayer, praise, trust in God, and active imitation of his free mercy; that it encourages the use of means in the highest degree; that it is ascertained by its effects in all who [truly] believe the gospel; [that it] is the foundation of Christian assurance; and that to ascertain it with regard to ourselves, demands and deserves our utmost diligence.

X. OF SANCTIFICATION.

[Added in 1853.]

We believe that sanctification is the process by which, according to the will of God, we are made partakers of his holiness; that it is a progressive work; that it is begun in regeneration; and that it is carried on in the hearts of believers by the presence and power of the Holy Spirit, the Sealer and Comforter, in the continual use of the appointed means—especially the Word of God, self-examination, self-denial, watchfulness and prayer.

XI. OF THE PERSEVERANCE OF SAINTS.

[We believe] That such only are real believers as endure unto the end; that their persevering attachment to Christ is the grand mark which distinguishes them from mere professors; that a special Providence watches over their welfare; and [that] they are kept by the power of God through faith unto salvation.

XII. [OF THE] HARMONY OF THE LAW AND THE GOSPEL.

[We believe] That the Law of God is the eternal and unchangeable rule of his moral government; that it is holy, just, and good; and that the inability which the Scriptures ascribe to fallen men to fulfill its precepts, arises entirely from their love of sin; to deliver them from which, and to restore them through a Mediator to unfeigned obedience to the holy law, is one great end of the Gospel, and of the means of grace connected with the establishment of the visible church.

XIII. OF A GOSPEL CHURCH.

[We believe] That a visible church of Christ is a congregation of baptized believers, associated by covenant in the faith and fellowship of the Gospel; observing the ordinances of Christ; governed by his laws; and exercising the gifts, rights, and privileges invested in them by his word; that its only proper officers are bishops or pastors, and deacons, whose qualifications, claims, and duties are defined in the Epistles to Timothy and Titus.

XIV. OF BAPTISM AND THE LORD'S SUPPER.

[We believe] That Christian baptism is the immersion of a believer in water, in the name of the Father [and] Son, and Spirit, to show forth in a solemn and beautiful emblem, our

faith in a crucified, buried, and risen
Savior, with its purifying power; that it is prerequisite to the privileges of a church relation;
and to the Lord's Supper, in which the members of the church, by the [sacred] use of bread
and wine, are to commemorate together the
dying love of Christ; preceded always by solemn self-examination.

XV. OF THE CHRISTIAN SABBATH.

[We believe] That the first day of the week
is the Lord's day, or Christian Sabbath; and is
to be kept sacred to religious purposes, by ab-
staining from all secular labor and [sinful]
recreations; by the devout observance of all
the means of grace, both private and public;
and by preparation for that rest which re-
maineth for the people of God.

XVI. OF CIVIL GOVERNMENT.

[We believe] That civil government is of
divine appointment, for the interests and good
order of human society; and that magistrates
are to be prayed for, conscientiously honored,
and obeyed, except [only] in things opposed
to the will of our Lord Jesus Christ, who is
the only Lord of the conscience, and the Prince
of the kings of the earth.

XVII. OF THE RIGHTEOUS AND THE WICKED.

[We believe] That there is a radical and essential difference between the righteous and the wicked; that such only as through faith are justified in the name of the Lord Jesus, and sanctified by the Spirit of our God, are truly righteous in his esteem; while all such as continue in impenitence and unbelief are in his sight wicked, and under the curse; and this distinction holds among men both in and after death.

XVIII. OF THE WORLD TO COME.

[We believe] That the end of this world is approaching: that at the last day Christ will descend from Heaven, and raise the dead from the grave to final retribution; that a solemn separation will then take place; that the wicked will be judged to endless punishment, and the righteous to endless joy; and that this judgment will fix forever the final state of men in Heaven or hell, on principles of righteousness.

A CHURCH COVENANT.

BY J. NEWTON BROWN.

Having been led, as we believe, by the Spirit of God, to receive the Lord Jesus Christ as our Savior, and on the profession of our faith, having been baptized in the name of our Father, and of the Son, and of the Holy Ghost, we do now in the presence of God, angels, and this assembly, most solemnly and joyfully enter into covenant with one another as one body in Christ.

We engage, therefore, by the aid of the Holy Spirit, to walk together in Christian love; to strive for the advancement of this church, in knowledge, holiness, and comfort, to promote its prosperity and spirituality; to sustain its worship, ordinances, discipline and doctrines, to contribute cheerfully and regularly to the support of the ministry, the expenses of the church, the relief of the poor, and the spread of the Gospel through all nations.

We also engage to maintain family and secret devotion; to religiously educate our children, to seek the salvation of our kindred and acquaintances, to walk circumspectly in the world, to be just in our dealings, faithful in our engagements and exemplary in our deportment, to avoid all tattling, backbiting and excessive anger, to abstain from the sale and use of intoxicating drinks as a beverage, and to be zealous in our efforts to advance the Kingdom of our Savior.

We further engage to watch over one another with brotherly love, to remember each other in prayer, to aid each other in sickness and distress, to cultivate Christian sympathy in feeling and courtesy in speech, to be slow to take offense, but always ready for reconciliation, and mindful of the rules of our Savior to secure it without delay.

We moreover engage that when we remove from this place, we will as soon as possible unite with some other church, where we can carry out the spirit of this covenant and the principles of God's word.

CHURCH COVENANT

BY E. T. HISCOX.

Having been, as we trust, brought by divine grace to embrace the Lord Jesus Christ, and to give ourselves wholly to him, we do now solemnly and joyfully covenant with each other to walk together in him, with brotherly love, to his glory, as our common Lord. We do, therefore, in his strength, engage—

That we will exercise a Christian watchfulness over each other, and faithfully warn, exhort, and admonish each other as occasion may require:

That we will not forsake the assembling of ourselves together, but will uphold the public worship of God and the ordinances of his house:

That we will not omit closet and family religion at home, nor neglect the great duty of religiously training our children, and those under our care, for the service of Christ and the enjoyment of Heaven:

That, as we are the light of the world, and the salt of the earth, we will seek divine aid, to enable us to deny ungodliness and every worldly lust, and to walk circumspectly in the world, that we may win the souls of men:

That we will cheerfully contribute of our property, according as God has prospered us, for the maintenance of a faithful and evangelical ministry among us, for the support of the poor, and to spread the Gospel over the earth:

That we will in all conditions, even till death, strive to live to the glory of him who hath called us out of darkness into his marvelous light.

"And may the God of peace, who brought again from the dead our Lord Jesus, that great Shepherd of the sheep, through the blood of the everlasting covenant, make us perfect in every good work to do his will, working in us that which is well pleasing in his sight through Jesus Christ, to whom be glory, for ever and ever. Amen."